FANTASTIC SCIENCE JOURNEYS

A TRIP THROUGH THE MILKY WAY

BY HEATHER MOORE NIVER

Gareth Stevens
PUBLISHING

Please visit our website, www.garethstevens.com. For a free color catalog of all our high-quality books, call toll free 1-800-542-2595 or fax 1-877-542-2596.

Library of Congress Cataloging-in-Publication Data

Niver, Heather Moore.
A trip through the Milky Way / by Heather Moore Niver.
p. cm. — (Fantastic science journeys)
Includes index.
ISBN 978-1-4824-2071-5 (pbk.)
ISBN 978-1-4824-2070-8 (6-pack)
ISBN 978-1-4824-2072-2 (library binding)
1. Milky Way — Juvenile literature. I. Niver, Heather Moore. II. Title.
QB857.7 N58 2015
523.1—d23

Published in 2015 by
Gareth Stevens Publishing
111 East 14th Street, Suite 349
New York, NY 10003

Copyright © 2015 Gareth Stevens Publishing

Designer: Sarah Liddell
Editor: Ryan Nagelhout

Photo credits: Cover, p. 1 Christopher Universe/Wikimedia Commons; p. 5 Kevin Key/Shutterstock.com; p. 7 photo courtesy of Nasa JPL; p. 9 Mopic/Shutterstock.com; p. 11 Mihai-Bogdan Lazar/Shutterstock.com; p. 13 Stocktrek Images/Getty Images; p. 15 photo courtesy of NASA/JPL-Caltech; p. 17 Stas1995/Wikimedia Commons; p. 19 Steve Allen/Getty Images; p. 21 Corey Ford/Stocktrek Images/Getty Images; p. 23 photo courtesy of ASA, ESA, SSC, CXC, and STSci; p. 25 photo courtesy of NASA, ESA, Z. Levay and R. van der Marel, STSci, T. Hallas, and A. Mellinger; p. 27 Diego Barucco/Shutterstock.com; p. 29 (Hubble) John Brenneis/Contributor/Getty Images; p. 29 (main) bikeriderlondon/Shutterstock.com.

Printed in the United States of America

CPSIA compliance information: Batch #CW15GS: For further information contact Gareth Stevens, New York, New York at 1-800-542-2595.

CONTENTS

Words in the glossary appear in **bold** type the first time they are used in the text.

UP, UP, AND AWAY!

Most of us have stared up on a dark night and watched the sky with bewilderment. There are so many stars, **planets**, and moons up there! And of course we see the sun—and sometimes the moon and other planets—during the day. There's so much to see!

Humans have gone into space, but what if we could fly anywhere in space we wanted? Let's climb aboard a special spaceship and fly far across our Milky Way **galaxy**!

THAT'S FANTASTIC!

In addition to the Milky Way, other galaxies can be seen from Earth. Just south of the **equator**, you can see the Large Magellanic Cloud and the Small Magellanic Cloud. They're named after the explorer Ferdinand Magellan.

The Milky Way is called a barred spiral galaxy, named for its whirling arms and the bar shape across the middle of it.

5

MYSTERIOUS MILKY WAY

A galaxy is made up of stars, gases, and dust that move through the universe together. As we speed through the night sky in our ship, we see a wide band of light. That's the center of the Milky Way!

The Milky Way is one of billions of galaxies in our universe! The sun and its planets, including Earth, are all part of the Milky Way. It contains more than 200 billion stars along with dust and gas. Almost all stars belong to galaxies.

THAT'S FANTASTIC!

The biggest galaxies hardly have any gas or dust. They can have more than 1 trillion stars, though. Our galaxy rotates, or spins around, about once every 200 million years.

The planet Earth is about halfway between the edge and the center of the Milky Way galaxy.

Earth

GALAXIES GREAT AND SMALL

As we travel farther and farther from Earth, we see the other planets in our **solar system**. There are two planets between Earth and the sun, Mercury and Venus. After Earth, there are five more planets, including the gas giant Jupiter.

There's a band of big rocks between Mars and Jupiter called an asteroid belt. Our solar system also has moons, comets, and other bodies circling around the sun.

THAT'S FANTASTIC!

Neptune, the eighth planet, is about 2.8 billion miles (4.5 billion km) from the sun.

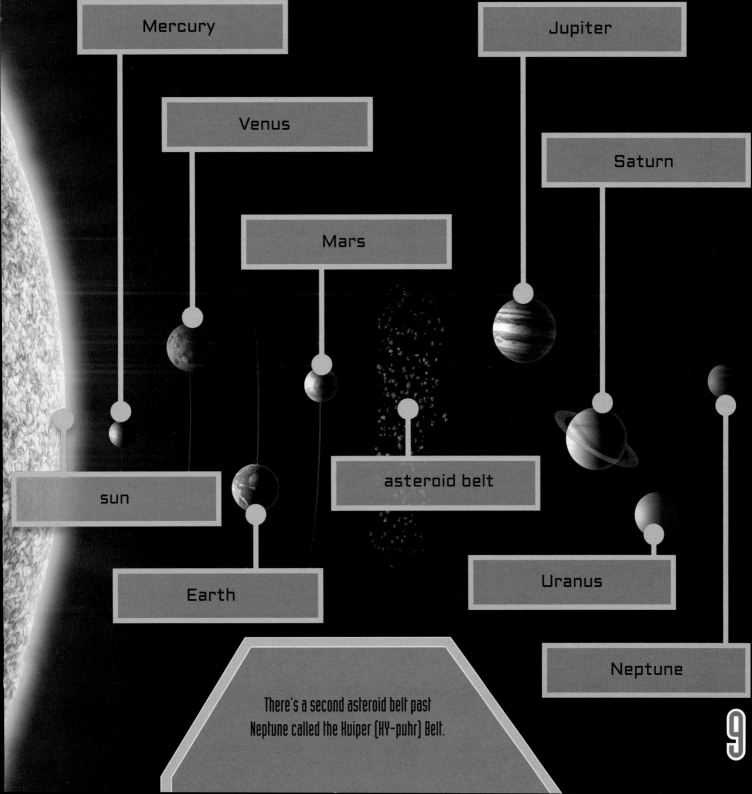

Mercury

Jupiter

Venus

Saturn

Mars

sun

asteroid belt

Earth

Uranus

Neptune

There's a second asteroid belt past
Neptune called the Kuiper (KY-puhr) Belt.

9

WHEN THEY WERE BORN

Galaxies were formed only a few million years after the universe was born. That was 13 billion years ago! At first, galaxies were much smaller than they are now. They've been growing ever since!

Most galaxies are in small clusters, or groups. The Milky Way is one of about 40 galaxies in what's called the Local Group. Let's take a quick side trip over the Local Group for perspective. We notice that the Andromeda Galaxy is the biggest in our cluster. The Milky Way and Andromeda are both spiral galaxies.

THAT'S FANTASTIC!

Even a small galaxy is really very big. It contains millions of stars! Small galaxies can be 5,000 **light-years** wide.

Galaxies in the Local Group all move together, like a big family!

Andromeda

As we leave the Milky Way behind, we start to see galaxies of all shapes and sizes. **Elliptical** galaxies are the largest. They are oval or shaped like a football. **Irregular** galaxies are uncommon and don't really have a set shape.

Spiral galaxies such as the Milky Way are shaped like pinwheels. Older stars are near the center. New stars are created from the dust and gas found in the pinwheel's arms. Earth is found at the end of one of the arms.

THAT'S FANTASTIC!

Light can pass through the Milky Way from one side to the other, but it takes 100,000 years because the galaxy is so big. That means the Milky Way is 100,000 light-years across!

elliptical galaxy

spiral galaxy

irregular galaxy

The shape of a galaxy is often affected by other nearby galaxies.

13

ARMS OF THE GALAXY

Now let's get back to our Milky Way adventure. It's not easy to map out the Milky Way because it's so large. The Milky Way has two to four spiral arms that start at a central bar. The Milky Way has smaller bars and spurs, or branches, too.

Scientists think the arms are created by waves that move through the galaxy, causing gas and dust to clump together in places. And in the middle of all this is one of the biggest mysteries yet: a **black hole**. We'll talk more about that later.

THAT'S FANTASTIC!

The Milky Way is just one of billions of spiral galaxies in the universe!

MAPPING THE MILKY WAY

Perseus main arm

Earth

black hole

outer arm

Scutum-Centaurus main arm

Earth's orbit

ON THE SIDE: A HOT HALO

Let's fly our ship over and take a look at the galaxy from the side. The Milky Way's arms make a flat disk. At the center is a "galactic bulge." It's stuffed so full of stars, gas, and dust that it blocks our view of stars in it and on the other side of the Milky Way.

The bulge and arms are the most eye-catching parts of the Milky Way, but it also has a round **halo** made of hot gas, old stars, and **globular clusters**. This halo is so big that it stretches for light-years.

THAT'S FANTASTIC!

Above and below the disk are two giant bubbles. The bubbles each have a **jet** of matter that's 27,000 light-years long!

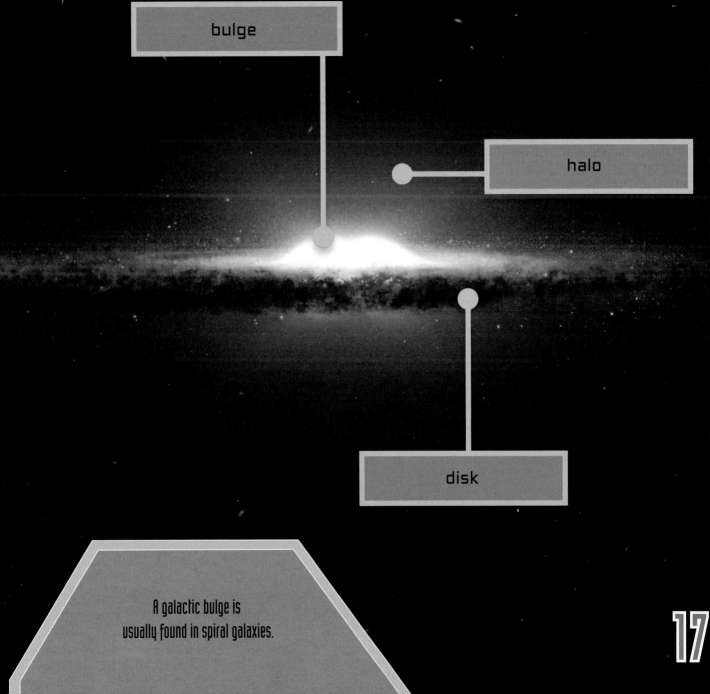

bulge

halo

disk

A galactic bulge is
usually found in spiral galaxies.

17

THE DEEP, DARK SECRET

Scientists have a challenge when studying what's at the very center of the Milky Way. Lots of dust clouds and gas make it hard to see exactly what's there.

What scientists think is at the center of the Milky Way is called a supermassive black hole. Black holes have superstrong **gravity**. So, they can be studied by looking at how things react to the pull of gravity when they get close to the black hole.

THAT'S FANTASTIC!

In 2014, scientists discovered a galaxy that has not one but three supermassive black holes at its center!

black hole

Black holes get their name because
they're invisible. Light can't escape from them.
Most galaxies probably have one in the middle, but we
can't see the one in the Milky Way from our ship.

HUNGRY, HUNGRY BLACK HOLE!

The Milky Way's black hole started out much smaller than it is now. Thanks to gravity, it keeps pulling in more objects and getting bigger. Scientists think this black hole gobbles up anything that gets close to it. So it might snack on dust, gas, stars, and even asteroids!

From our ship, we can see bright flares, or flashes of light, around the black hole. These light shows can last up to an hour!

THAT'S FANTASTIC!

Some astronomers call the black hole a monster because it eats up so much stuff! They think it's very destructive.

The light show near the black hole comes from gas clouds being trapped inside.

DEEP DARK MATTER

So far, we've seen that the Milky Way is chock full of dust, gas, and stars. But there's even more to our galaxy than that. It's also made up of dark matter.

Unfortunately, we can't see dark matter from our special ship. That's because it's invisible. This means we aren't sure what it's made of! Scientists have to study the objects around it, like they do with black holes, and notice how they act. Dark matter makes up about 90 percent of the Milky Way.

THAT'S FANTASTIC!

Scientists say that dark matter forms a halo around the Milky Way.

Scientists are still trying to understand dark matter and what it does to the Milky Way.

23

MILKY WAY MASH-UP

With space full of galaxies, it's probably not a big surprise to learn that they run into each other. But it's shocking to know that they actually smash into each other all the time! That goes for the Milky Way, too!

We can't see it from our ship, but scientists think the Milky Way will run into the Andromeda Galaxy in about 4 billion years. These two galaxies are speeding toward each other at about 70 miles (112 km) per second! Scientists say Andromeda has smashed into other galaxies in the past.

THAT'S FANTASTIC!

When galaxies crash into each other, all kinds of matter comes together to create a whole new star formation!

Andromeda

Milky Way

The Andromeda Galaxy is
2.5 million light-years away, but you can
see it from Earth, sometimes even without binoculars.

ALIEN EARTHS

From the window of our ship, we see a red dwarf star. Most of the stars in the Milky Way are called red dwarfs. They're smaller than the sun—about one-tenth its size. Red dwarfs are also cooler than the sun and less bright.

There are about 4.5 billion red dwarfs in the Milky Way. The red dwarf that's closest to Earth is about 12 light-years away. Scientists think there could be other life living near these stars on planets much like Earth!

THAT'S FANTASTIC!

When they're first "born," red dwarf stars explode a lot. So scientists aren't sure if they'd be the best stars to live near!

Red dwarf stars live longer than our sun, which is a yellow dwarf star, will last.

GAZING AT THE GALAXY

In the 1920s, astronomer Edwin Hubble realized there was more than one galaxy in space. Scientists had thought all the stars were part of the Milky Way. Scientists still have plenty to learn about our galaxy. But they are always hard at work on new ways to measure and figure out the exact shape of it.

Now that we've taken a look at the Milky Way, it's time to cruise back to Earth in our spaceship. We sure have a lot to think about when we look at the sky at night!

THAT'S FANTASTIC!

More than 200 billion stars call the Milky Way home! And there's enough matter in this galaxy to make billions more stars!

Edwin Hubble also figured out that the universe was constantly getting bigger.

Edwin Hubble

GLOSSARY

black hole: a huge amount of matter packed in a tiny space, with such strong gravity nothing can get out

elliptical: having an oval or football shape

equator: the imaginary line that circles the middle of Earth

galaxy: a large group of stars, planets, gas, and dust that form a unit within the universe

globular cluster: a ball-shaped group of stars

gravity: a force that pulls objects toward the center of a planet or star

halo: a circle of light that shines around a planet or galaxy

irregular: not even or balanced

jet: a powerful rush of matter through a narrow space

light-year: the distance light can travel in 1 year

planet: a large object in space that circles a star

solar system: the sun and all the space objects that orbit it, including the planets and their moons

FOR MORE INFORMATION

BOOKS

Coupe, Robert. *Earth's Place in Space*. New York, NY: PowerKids Press, 2014.

Rustad, Martha E. H. *The Milky Way*. North Mankato, MN: Capstone Press, 2012.

World Book. *The Milky Way*. Chicago, IL: World Book, 2010.

WEBSITES

Catalogue of the Cosmos
pbs.org/wgbh/nova/space/catalogue-cosmos.html
Check out this site if you're curious to learn more about amazing astronomical objects.

Space Facts: Galaxy Facts for Kids
sciencekids.co.nz/sciencefacts/space/galaxies.html
Rocket on over to this site for more fun galaxy facts and information!

INDEX